WE THE PEOPLE

The Salem Witch Trials

by Michael Burgan

Content Adviser: Dr. Alan Rogers, History Department Chair,
Boston College, Boston, Massachusetts

Reading Adviser: Susan Kesselring, M.A., Literacy Educator,
Rosemount-Apple Valley-Eagan (Minnesota) School District

COMPASS POINT BOOKS
MINNEAPOLIS, MINNESOTA

Compass Point Books
151 Good Counsel Drive
P.O. Box 669
Mankato, MN 56002-0669

Visit Compass Point Books on the Internet at *www.compasspointbooks.com*
or e-mail your request to *custserv@compasspointbooks.com*

On the cover: A girl is accused of witchcraft in Salem, Massachusetts, in 1692.

Photographs ©: Bettmann/Corbis, cover, 20, 30; Prints Old and Rare, back cover (left); Library of Congress, back cover; Stock Montage, Inc., 5, 11 (right); Hulton Archive/Getty Images, 6, 10, 12, 33; North Wind Picture Archives, 7, 8, 9, 15, 21, 23, 24, 26, 29, 34, 40; Photodisc, 11 (left); Courtesy of the Massachusetts Historical Society, 17; Courtesy of Salem Witch Museum, 18; Baldwin H. Ward & Kathryn C. Ward/Corbis, 22; Lee Snider/Corbis, 31; F. A. Carter, 32; Wildside Press, 35; Bill Bachmann/Index Stock Imagery, 37; Courtesy Danvers Archival Center, Danvers, Mass., 39.

Creative Director: Terri Foley
Managing Editor: Catherine Neitge
Editor: Brenda Haugen
Photo Researcher: Marcie C. Spence
Designer/Page production: Bradfordesign, Inc./Les Tranby
Cartographer: XNR Productions, Inc
Educational Consultant: Diane Smolinski

Library of Congress Cataloging-in-Publication Data
Burgan, Michael.
  The Salem witch trials / by Michael Burgan.
  Includes bibliographical references and index.
  ISBN-13: 978-0-7565-0845-6 (hardcover)
  ISBN-10: 0-7565-0845-2 (hardcover)
  1. Trials (Witchcraft)-Massachusetts-Salem-History-17th century-Juvenile literature. 2. Witchcraft-Massachusetts-Salem-History-17th century-Juvenile literature. I. Title. II. We the people (Series) (Compass Point Books)
  KFM2478.8.W5B87 2004
  133.4'3'097445-dc22   2004016309

TABLE OF CONTENTS

A Hunt for Witches

Sometime around January 20, 1692, a mysterious sickness struck 11-year-old Abigail Williams and her young cousin Betty Parris. A minister in their community wrote that the girls looked as if they had been "bitten and pinched by invisible agents." Their arms and backs twisted in unnatural ways, "beyond the power of any ... natural disease to effect." A town doctor soon declared that the girls were bewitched. Two more girls in the same community showed similar signs of being under a witch's spell.

The four girls lived in Salem, an important seaport in Massachusetts. In 1692, many people in Massachusetts and in other American colonies believed that witches were real. Witches were men and women who were said to make deals with Satan, another name for the devil. People promised to worship Satan and work for him. In return, people believed that Satan gave them special powers, such as the ability to fly or cast harmful spells on their enemies.

A woman imprisoned for witchcraft is confronted by her persecutors.

The bewitched girls of Salem began to accuse people in the town of being witches. Other people also stepped forward and said they were afflicted or they knew people who were witches. Panic spread across Salem and into nearby towns. People wondered who was a witch and who might be afflicted next. Even wealthy and highly respected citizens were accused of witchcraft.

William Stoughton served as lead judge.

Witchcraft was a crime in Massachusetts and in most European countries. Convicted witches were killed. By the summer of 1692, dozens of people in and around Salem were in jail and facing trial for witchcraft. During the Salem witch trials, 19 people were convicted of being witches. All were executed by hanging.

Many more people might have died, except some people in the colony began to doubt that so many people could be witches. Massachusetts governor William Phips finally stepped in and ended some of the trials. He later pardoned several people accused of witchcraft.

Historians believe the girls of Salem were not afflicted by witchcraft. They also believe the convicted

6

A young woman reads the Bible in jail in New England in the 1600s.

people were not actually witches. Historians today think it was fear that fueled the panic in Salem and made the townspeople accuse innocent people of being witches.

Some residents of Salem were afraid that traditional Puritan beliefs were becoming unpopular. Devoted Christians worried that God and the Bible would have less influence over their community. They believed the devil was one source of this problem.

7

Native Americans fight with settlers in New England in the 1600s.

Possibly adding to their fear were the battles with Native Americans that were happening in nearby New Hampshire and southern Maine. Some people in Salem were concerned Native Americans might attack them, too.

8

The Salem witch trials were not the first time that innocent people were wrongly accused of being witches. But they were part of the largest and deadliest "witch hunt" in American history.

A trial for witchcraft in Salem in 1692

SALEM'S PURITAN ROOTS

The town of Salem was first settled in 1626. English Puritans arrived about two years later.

The Puritans settled in Massachusetts so they could worship as they chose. They wanted to purify, or improve, the Church of England, which was that country's official church. In England, the Puritans did not have the power to purify the church as they wanted. So Puritan leaders decided they would create their own churches and government in Massachusetts. They would rule based on their religious ideas. The Puritans hoped their colony would be so

Puritan colonists on their way to church

Puritans followed the teachings of the Bible.

A painting of Jesus Christ and some of his followers

successful that the English would finally accept their ideas and beliefs.

The Puritans believed that God chose a certain number of people to go to heaven after they died. During their lives, these elect were supposed to follow the teachings of Jesus Christ and other rules outlined in the Bible. The

Puritans said that even people who were not part of the elect should act as if they were. All people should live moral lives and hope they were among the lucky few who would go to heaven.

A painting of Satan waking his troops

The Puritans, like other Christians of the time, believed that Satan was real. He was an angel who rebelled against God and spread evil on Earth. The Puritans thought that Satan tried to make people disobey God and the teachings in the Bible. They believed witches were the devil's servants and helped him carry out his wicked work. Puritan ministers said that women were especially likely to become witches. The ministers believed that women were morally weak. They said women could be more easily tempted to reject God and worship Satan.

To the Puritans, a person who practiced witchcraft was an enemy of God and a danger to Christians. In 1641, England passed a law making witchcraft illegal. England ruled over Massachusetts and the other colonies, so English laws applied in the colonies, too.

In general, colonial officials did not often convict and execute people for witchcraft. The leaders knew that people might falsely accuse others of being witches. Finding solid proof of witchcraft was hard. Some people also began to consider witchcraft a superstition, not something based on facts. In Salem, however, the conditions were right for the fear of witches to spread.

TROUBLES IN SALEM

By the 1690s, the community of Salem had two parts.
A group of families lived in northwest Salem in an area
called Salem Village. Most families lived in southeast
Salem in an area known as Salem Town.

The residents of Salem Village were in conflict in the
early 1690s. Some of the local farmers in the west end of

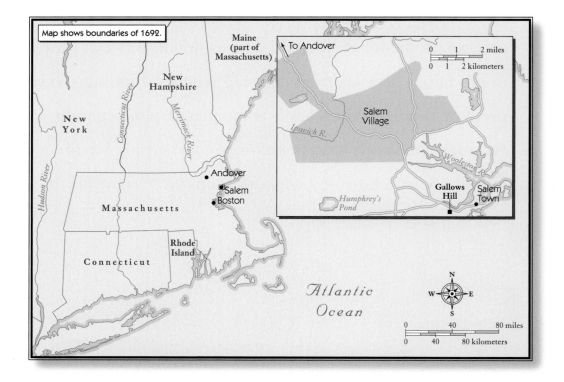

the village wanted to form their own community separate from Salem. Most of the people living in the east end of Salem Village had jobs tied to Salem Town's sea trade. They wanted to keep the community together. The argument over whether to form a new town upset many of those living in Salem.

Some people saw the disagreement as a religious issue. The Salem Village farmers thought citizens on the east side of Salem Village and the Salem Town residents

Merchant ships sail into a harbor to trade with colonists.

did not truly follow Puritan teachings. For decades, the strong faith of the first Puritan settlers had been weakening. After the original settlers had arrived, people who were not Puritans began settling in Massachusetts. Some of the newcomers seemed more interested in making money than in living a moral life. Even some Puritans lost their strong religious faith. This worried the strict Puritans. The west-end residents of Salem Village thought they were better Puritans than their neighbors, so they wanted to form their own town.

In 1689, a few wealthy families in western Salem Village decided to form their own congregation, separate from the old church that Salem Puritans attended. For these Salem Village residents, forming their own church was an important step to becoming a separate town. They hired Samuel Parris as their minister.

At the time, part of the taxes collected in Massachusetts towns was used to pay ministers' salaries. The people who hired Parris also gave him his own house and the land around it. Salem Village residents who opposed separating from Salem Town disliked giving Parris such generous benefits. They protested by refusing to attend his religious services and pay their taxes.

Samuel Parris

The disagreement about Parris and the separation issue went on for two years. In 1691, village residents who opposed Parris won local elections. They refused to collect taxes to pay Parris's salary. The new leaders also challenged his right to own the home he had been given two years before. Parris found himself caught between two warring sides. He had to rely on charity from his supporters in the west end so he and his family could survive.

17

THE FIRST ACCUSED "WITCHES"

No one knows what caused the fits that afflicted Samuel Parris's niece Abigail and his daughter Betty in 1692. The two girls, however, blamed the family's slave Tituba for bewitching them. Tituba admitted that she had learned some things about witchcraft, such as spells,

Tituba talks to Betty Parris and Betty Williams in the Parris kitchen.

from a previous owner. However, she insisted she was not a witch.

Still, two more afflicted girls soon stepped forward and accused Tituba of witchcraft. They also named two more local women as witches.

One of the accused was Sarah Good. Her neighbors had earlier claimed that she was a witch. They accused her of bewitching them and their animals, but she had not been arrested.

The second woman who was accused of being a witch was Sarah Osborne. She and her husband were involved in a legal dispute with Thomas Putnam. His family had led the efforts to make Salem's two areas—Salem Village and Salem Town—two separate communities. Putnam's daughter Ann was one of the afflicted girls.

On February 29, 1692, Thomas Putnam and several other men in Salem Village visited local officials. The men formally accused Tituba, Sarah Good, and Sarah Osborne

19

Sarah Osborne's house

of witchcraft. The accused witches were then questioned about their actions. Sarah Good denied that she was a witch and that she had harmed the afflicted girls. But she accused Sarah Osborne of witchcraft. Osborne denied that charge, and she suggested that perhaps the devil made himself look like her when he did his evil business.

The most shocking moments of the questioning came from Tituba. She admitted that "the devil came to me and bid me to serve him." She described how Satan sometimes appeared as a dog or a hog. Other times, she

Copies of statements to the court from Ann Putnam
and another girl on May 31, 1692

saw black cats and rats. Tituba also said that she, Osborne,

and Good had signed a book in blood, showing that they

had made a deal with the devil. Throughout the

questioning of all three women, the four afflicted girls

continued to claim that the accused women were witches.

The news of Tituba's statements soon spread around

Salem. Other people in town then began to say that they

had seen ghostly images of Osborne, Good, and Tituba.

The afflicted girls also talked about similar specters, or

Townspeople accuse a woman of witchcraft.

ghosts, that flew around and tried to hurt them. They also accused more people of being witches. Ann Putnam made many of these charges. She described how one local woman "did often appear to her and torture her by pinching and other ways."

As people were accused of witchcraft, they were arrested and thrown in jail. There they would wait until their trials if they didn't confess to being witches.

THE PANIC SPREADS

In late March 1692, Deodat Lawson came to speak in Salem Village. Lawson had served as a minister in Salem several years before. Lawson talked about the devil's work in Salem. He said that since God was all-powerful, he had allowed Satan to come into the town and harm the girls. God was punishing the town because they had disobeyed his teachings.

A few days later, Samuel Parris spoke to the members of his congregation. He said that anyone could be a devil—even someone who seemed to be a faithful follower of Jesus Christ. Lawson's and Parris's ideas may have influenced the thinking of the residents of Salem. They became even

A child accuses a man of witchcraft.

more suspicious about their neighbors. Anyone around them could be a witch.

By the middle of April, two more women had joined Tituba and confessed to being witches. One of them was a teenager named Abigail Hobbs. She was one of the first alleged witches who did not live in Salem Village. From this point on, more of the accused witches came from beyond the village. Many lived in the nearby town of Andover.

A Modest Enquiry

Into the Nature of

Witchcraft,

AND

How Persons Guilty of that Crime may be *Convicted* : And the means used for their Discovery Discussed, both *Negatively* and *Affirmatively*. according to *SCRIPTURE* and *EXPERIENCE.*

By John Hale,

Pastor of the Church of Christ in *Beverley,* Anno Domini 1697.

When they say unto you, seek unto them that have Familiar Spirits and unto Wizzards, that peep, &c. To the Law and to the Testimony ; if they speak not according to this word, it is because there is no light in them, Isaiah VIII. 19, 20. *That which I see not teach thou me,* Job 34 32.

BOSTON in N. E.

Printed by *B. Green,* and *J. Allen,* for *Benjamin Eliot* under the Town House. 1702

Books about witchcraft could easily be found in the 1600s.

24

At her confession, Hobbs said, "I have been very wicked." She explained that the devil took her shape and hurt the afflicted people who had accused her.

As Hobbs spoke, Abigail Williams, Ann Putnam, and several other girls said they saw ghostly images of Sarah Good and Sarah Osborne. Hobbs said the specters stuck their fingers in her ears so she could not hear the questions the officials asked her.

Hobbs said that she had first met the devil three or four years earlier, when she lived on the Maine frontier. At that time, the area that is today the state of Maine was part of Massachusetts. Starting in 1689, the Wabanaki Indians had begun to attack New England settlers along the frontier. Hobbs was the first of many people involved in the Salem witch trials who had some connection to the fighting there.

A recent historical study suggests that some of the afflicted people connected the devil with the Indians. This idea had deep roots in Puritan thinking. Ministers often

New England colonists arrest an accused witch in the 1600s.

said that New England had been filled with evil before Christianity arrived there. They believed the Native Americans did the devil's work, unless they became Christians. People who had seen Indian attacks or feared them seemed more likely to think the devil was recruiting witches in and around Salem.

After Hobbs confessed, the number of people accused of witchcraft quickly rose. More than 50 were accused during the next two months.

The first man had also been accused by this time. His name was John Proctor. He had protested when his wife, Elizabeth, was questioned. He said he believed that some of the accusers were lying.

People who questioned the witch hunt sometimes faced charges that they were also witches. Few people risked speaking out against the search for the devil's work.

THE TRIALS BEGIN

In late May, Massachusetts Governor Phips called for a court to meet in Salem and decide if the accused people were actually witches. The judges included the lieutenant governor of Massachusetts and other important men in the colony.

All of the judges had somehow been connected to the recent violence with the Indians in and around Maine. They might have believed the devil had influenced both the Wabanaki and the accused witches. Or they might have wanted to direct people's attention away from the Indian raids—and the fact that they and other leaders had been unable to stop them.

Tituba and other confessed witches did not have to go to court. Under English law, witches were not allowed to speak in court. Officials believed they could not be trusted to speak the truth, since they did not worship God.

28

Confessed witches therefore avoided the death sentence, although they had to stay in jail. Only convicted witches who did not admit their crimes were killed. This fact helps explain why more people who were innocent began to confess to being witches. They did not want to risk being found guilty in court and face death. Over time, however, some of the confessed witches later denied that they were witches.

The crowd reacts to a guilty verdict in one of the trials.

The witch trials started on June 2, 1692. The first person to appear before the court was Bridget Bishop. Years before, some residents had thought she might be a

29

Bridget Bishop is hanged for witchcraft.

witch. Now, several people said that she had come to them in spectral form. One accuser said Bishop "did appear … tempting her to sign the [devil's] book … and did torture and afflict" her. Again and again, Bishop insisted that she was not a witch. The jury did not

30

believe her, and she received a death sentence. About a week later, she was hanged. She was the first alleged witch to be executed.

The home of Rebecca Nurse

By the end of June, five more people had been found guilty of witchcraft. These included Rebecca Nurse, a 71-year-old grandmother. Most residents of Salem considered her to be a loving, faithful woman. Yet Abigail Williams and others said that Nurse had afflicted them. During the trial, the afflicted often cried out, saying that Nurse was tormenting them even in the courtroom.

Nurse's family collected signatures from people who swore she was a good Christian. The family also tried to show that some of the accusers could not be trusted.

On June 30, the jury found Nurse not guilty, which set off an uproar in the courtroom. The judge, one observer

Rebecca Nurse is brought in chains in front of her church congregation.

wrote, also seemed "strangely surprised" by the verdict. In general, the judges seemed ready to believe that the accused were actually witches. One judge asked the jury to reconsider its verdict. When the jury asked Nurse a question, she did not respond—most likely because she had hearing problems and was also upset about the trial. The jury, however, assumed that she did not answer because she was truly guilty. This time, they convicted her of witchcraft and sentenced her to die.

This scene would be repeated again and again in the Salem courtroom. More accused witches were brought to trial, and more were sentenced to death.

IMPORTANT MINISTERS

The Salem witch trials caught the attention of several important people in Boston, where the colony of Massachusetts's government met. Increase Mather and his son Cotton were respected Congregationalist ministers there. (By 1689, the Puritans of Massachusetts were known as Congregationalists.) Both Increase and Cotton believed that Satan could influence human events, and Cotton had written a book about witchcraft.

Cotton Mather

"There are devils and witches," the younger Mather wrote, and "New England has had examples of their existence and operation." The devil appeared to the Indians, he said, and also to Christians.

Cotton Mather knew three of the judges in the Salem trials. He wrote a letter warning them not to rely

33

too much on spectral evidence. It was easy for the accused to claim they saw the specter of a witch. It was harder to prove that the specter existed.

Also, Mather said, Satan was powerful enough to send the specter of an innocent person to visit an afflicted person. Mather and others thought "devil's marks" were better signs of someone's being a witch. These marks included moles, pimples, and warts that somehow looked unnatural. Also, if bruises on an accused person's body matched ones seen on a specter, the person was likely a witch.

In general, Mather said the judges should act quickly. That speed, some historians say,

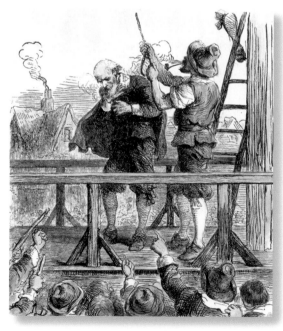

An old man is hanged as a witch.

led to so many innocent people being found guilty of witchcraft.

While some ministers talked about what proof could be found to convict a witch, one minister was being accused of being a witch himself. Congregationalist minister George Burroughs was

George Burroughs is arrested by the Salem sheriff in 1692.

convicted of witchcraft during the summer of 1692. Burroughs had once served in Salem Village. He left because of an argument with some residents about his salary. A relative of one of the people Burroughs quarreled with was one of his accusers in 1692.

Like Rebecca Nurse, Burroughs had many people who tried to defend him. But many more were ready to accuse him of witchcraft. Ann Putnam described how he "had made Abigail Hobbs a witch and several witches more; and he has continued ever since." Putnam and others accused Burroughs of being a leader of the witches. They said he had killed soldiers who fought the Indians and murdered his first two wives.

On August 19, Burroughs and Cotton Mather both stood on Gallows Hill. Convicted witches were hanged there. Mather wanted to see the execution of Burroughs and several other witches.

Before he died, Burroughs stunned the crowd by reciting a Christian prayer. The people of the time believed that a witch could not recite this prayer. Some people in the crowd thought that Burroughs might not be a witch after all. A few said that the execution should be stopped. Mather, however, pointed out that a jury had done its work and found Burroughs guilty. The execution went forward.

THE END OF THE WITCH HUNT

By the end of September 1692, 19 men and women had been hanged for being witches. Several alleged and confessed witches died while in jail.

Another accused witch died in a more gruesome way. Giles Corey was 80 years old and a longtime member of the Congregational Church. He refused to enter a plea to the charge of witchcraft. Instead, he stood silently. As punishment, Salem officials put a wooden board on Corey's chest as he lay on the ground. The officials piled stones on the board until the weight killed Corey.

Accused witches could not be buried in Salem cemeteries.

37

As the autumn of 1692 began, dozens of accused witches were still waiting to go on trial. By this time, people in Salem and Boston began to think that the Salem witch hunt had gone too far. Some leaders doubted that one small region of Massachusetts could have so many witches.

Increase Mather noted that the judges had ignored his son's warning not to use spectral evidence. He said, "It were better that 10 suspected witches should escape, than that one innocent person should be condemned."

The Mathers and others still believed in witches. However, they did not believe all the evidence that was being used in the Salem trials.

Other people thought the witch trials had gone too far after the executions of Rebecca Nurse and George Burroughs. They could not believe that two people who had always been good Christians would work for the devil. The death of Giles Corey also upset some residents of Salem.

Rebecca Nurse Memorial was built in 1885.

One of the harshest critics of the trials was Thomas Brattle. This Boston merchant was also a scientist. He thought the facts in some of the witch trials were weak. Brattle particularly disliked one test used to prove if a person were a witch. In this "touch test," an afflicted person touched an accused witch. People believed that the devil's power inside the victim would flow back into the accused witch. The victim would no longer be afflicted if the accused were actually a witch. Brattle argued that the touch test was not scientific. He wrote, "I am fully persuaded that is … a superstitious method, and that which we have no rule for, either from reason or religion."

William Phips

Brattle made his comments in a public letter that appeared in early October. By this time, other ministers had begun to speak out against the trials.

Within a few weeks, Governor Phips halted the arrest of alleged witches. He also freed many of the accused witches and closed down the court.

Lawmakers in Massachusetts called for a new court to hear the cases against the remaining alleged witches. In January 1693, almost all of them were freed because they had been accused based on spectral evidence. In May, Governor Phips pardoned all the remaining alleged witches.

The Salem witch trials marked the last major witch hunt in colonial America. However, their impact lasted for many years.

In 1702, Massachusetts lawmakers admitted that the legal system had failed during the witch trials. They said the trials were illegal.

Hysteria had let people believe that innocent people had done terrible things. Salem residents were split into different groups that did not always trust or like each other. Some people accused others of witchcraft because of personal disagreements. The threat of Indian attack also created a panic that led to accusations that may not have been based on facts or proof. All these things created an atmosphere that made accusations of witchcraft believable in Salem in 1692.

Today, Americans are still fascinated with the Salem witch trials. The idea that some people might have evil powers has not gone away. Most people, however, study the Salem witch trials because they explain something about human nature. Neighbors can turn against neighbors during difficult times. Wild ideas can easily spread among a wide group of people. The Salem affair showed the danger of letting feelings influence the court system.

Glossary

afflicted—ill or troubled in some way

alleged—accused of breaking a law but not yet found guilty

bewitched—under the influence of a witch

congregation—group of people who come together to form a church

convicted—found guilty of breaking the law

elect (as a noun)—someone chosen by God to go to heaven

execute—to kill as punishment for committing a crime

frontier—the distant edge of a settlement

hysteria—strong fear that spreads among a group of people

moral—relating to good behavior or thoughts

pardoned—legally forgiven for breaking a law

superstition—a folktale or belief not based on facts or science

DID YOU KNOW?

- Several young children were accused of witchcraft. The youngest was 4-year-old Dorcas Good, daughter of convicted witch Sarah Good. Dorcas was released from jail and did not go to trial.

- Scientists and historians have suggested several possible causes for the sickness that afflicted Abigail Williams and Betty Parris. These include various diseases or poisoning from a mold called Ergot found in the wheat. The wheat was ground and made into bread, infecting whoever ate it.

- By the time Governor Phips stopped the witch trials, even his wife had been accused of witchcraft.

- In 1752, Salem Village became the town of Danvers, Massachusetts.

- One 17th century historian reported that Tituba claimed Samuel Parris beat her so she would confess to being a witch. She later denied being a witch. Tituba was released from jail in 1693 and went to work for a new master.

- *The Crucible*, a well-known play and movie, is based on the Salem witch trials. Arthur Miller, the author of the play, was also the screenwriter for the movie.

IMPORTANT DATES

Timeline

1628	English Puritans start settling in Salem, Massachusetts.
1641	England passes a law banning witchcraft.
1689	Samuel Parris becomes the minister in Salem Village. Residents in the town are split over the idea of breaking away from the larger Salem Town and forming their own town.
1692	In January, Betty Parris and Abigail Williams show signs of a bizarre illness. In February, three women of Salem Village are accused of witchcraft. In June, the witch trials begin and Bridget Bishop is the first convicted witch to be executed. In September, the last of 19 hangings takes place. In October, Thomas Brattle publishes a letter attacking the witch trials, and Governor William Phips soon closes the court hearing the trials.
1693	In January, most of the alleged witches still in jail are freed. In May, Governor Phips pardons the rest of the accused witches.

IMPORTANT PEOPLE

GEORGE BURROUGHS (1650?-1692)
Former minister in Salem Village who was accused of witchcraft while living in Maine and executed in Salem

REBECCA NURSE (1621-1692)
Respected citizen of Salem who was executed for witchcraft

SAMUEL PARRIS (1653-1720)
Minister in Salem Village during the Salem witch trials; his daughter and niece were the first two people said to be bewitched

WILLIAM PHIPS (1651-1695)
Governor of Massachusetts who set up the first witch trials and later halted them

ANN PUTNAM (1680-1716)
Member of a powerful family in Salem Village and one of the main accusers of alleged witches

TITUBA (?)
A slave owned by Samuel Parris who confessed to being a witch

ABIGAIL WILLIAMS (1681?-?)
Niece of Samuel Parris and one of the first people in Salem to accuse others of witchcraft

WANT TO KNOW MORE?

At the Library

Boraas, Tracy. *The Salem Witch Trials*. Mankato, Minn.: Capstone Press, 2004.

Dolan, Edward F. *The Salem Witch Trials*. New York: Benchmark Books/Marshall Cavendish, 2002.

Lutz, Norma Jean. *Cotton Mather*. Philadelphia: Chelsea House Publishers, 2000.

On the Web

For more information on the *Salem witch trials*, use FactHound to track down Web sites related to this book.

1. Go to *www.facthound.com*.
2. Type in a search word related to this book or this book ID: 0756508452.
3. Click on the *Fetch It* button.

Your trusty Fact Hound will fetch the best Web sites for you!

On the Road

Salem Witch Trials Memorial

Charter Street

Salem, MA 01970

To visit the memorial that commemorates the 19 people executed for witchcraft

The Witch House

310 Essex St.

Salem, MA 01970

978/744-8815

To see one of the places where accused witches were questioned and learn more about the trials

Look for more We the People books about this era:

African-Americans in the Colonies

The California Missions

The French and Indian War

The Jamestown Colony

The Mayflower Compact

The Plymouth Colony

The Stamp Act of 1765

The Thirteen Colonies

Williamsburg

A complete list of We the People titles is available on our Web site:
www.compasspointbooks.com

INDEX

About the Author

Michael Burgan is a freelance writer for children and adults. A history graduate of the University of Connecticut, he has written more than 60 fiction and nonfiction children's books for various publishers. For adult audiences, he has written news articles, essays, and plays. Michael Burgan is a recipient of an Educational Press Association of America award and belongs to the Society of Children's Book Writers and Illustrators.